Building Powerful Strategic Alliances

How to Leverage Today's Most Effective Business-Building Strategy

John J. Bowen Jr.

Paul Brunswick

Jonathan J. Powell

Insights and Actions for Success

Dear Financial Advisor,

We are extremely pleased to be able to offer you some of the lessons we have learned from the top financial advisors we have had the privilege of working with.

Every year, we have the opportunity to lead workshops for thousands of financial advisors and to intensively coach hundreds more. We also conduct empirical research on financial advisors' best practices to uncover exactly what the most successful financial advisors in the industry are doing to build very profitable businesses while providing world-class service to their clients.

When we separate the very successful financial advisors from the less successful, we find a number of key success drivers. In *Building Powerful Strategic Alliances*, we will look at one of the most potent approaches we know to take your business to a significantly higher level in a relatively short period of time. Our goal? To enable you to substantially grow your practice while serving your clients extremely well.

Our reasons for doing so are simple. First, we want to give back to the industry that has provided our firm with so many opportunities. Second, we want to show you a small slice of what we offer to the elite financial advisors (and those aspiring to the elite level) in our coaching programs. If you like what you see, you may want to explore the opportunities we offer for working with a select group of financial advisors who want to break through to much higher levels of professional, financial and personal success, all while serving their affluent clients well.

Best of success,

John J. Bowen Jr.

John J. Bowen Jr.
Founder and CEO
CEG Worldwide, LLC

Building Powerful Strategic Alliances
How to Leverage Today's Most Effective Business-Building Strategy

CEG Worldwide, LLC • 1954 Hayes Lane • San Martin, CA 95046
(888) 551-3824 • www.cegworldwide.com • info@cegworldwide.com

Table of Contents

Introduction

SUCCESSFUL STRATEGIC ALLIANCES REQUIRE TIME AND diligence. But their potential reward is well worth the effort. Simply put, they are the most effective approach we know to take your business to a significantly higher level in a relatively short period of time.

We know—both through our industry research and through the work of hundreds of financial advisors in our coaching programs—that the majority of affluent clients prefer to find their financial advisors through referrals from trusted professionals. Well-crafted strategic alliances will create a stream of introductions to pre-qualified, affluent prospects from their professional advisors—your strategic partners.

Today's economic climate has created a number of business challenges for professional advisors. Many are looking for new ways to grow their practices and are turning to financial advisors for help in doing so. Through strategic alliances, they are able to grow their revenues at comparatively little cost and, just as important, to serve their clients better. This makes them preconditioned to want to work with financial advisors.

Our goal with this ebook and the companion videos is to give you the knowledge you need to systematically tap the potential of strategic alliances. You will learn what sets true strategic alliances apart from informal referral arrangements and how that difference will benefit both you and your strategic partners. So that you can see why strategic alliances are so attractive to other professionals, we will show you the results of a study we recently conducted of CPA firms that rely heavily on alliances with financial advisors.

To get you started on building powerful alliances, we will give you a method for assessing the strategic potential of any professional advisor to identify the best candidates. We then will delve into the strategic alliance consultative process—our road-tested method for building winning strategic partnerships. Finally, you will learn how to hit the ground running by using the three key best practices for strategic alliances.

Strategic alliances create that rarest of situations: a true win-win-win. Other professional advisors win by growing their revenues from their current client bases. Financial advisors win by acquiring additional affluent clients. And those clients win by receiving the complete range of financial services through a single trusted professional. We encourage you to explore how to create this win-win-win in your own business.

Why Strategic Alliances?

As a financial advisor, you may have found that referrals from other professionals are important for bringing qualified prospects into your practice. If so, you are far from alone. In a CEG Worldwide study of more than 2,000 financial advisors industry-wide, three out of five (61 percent) reported that such referrals were the source of their five best new clients in the previous year. Coming in a distant second were referrals from existing clients, cited by 23.4 percent of surveyed financial advisors. (See **Exhibit 1**.)

EXHIBIT 1
Source of Five Best New Clients in Previous Year

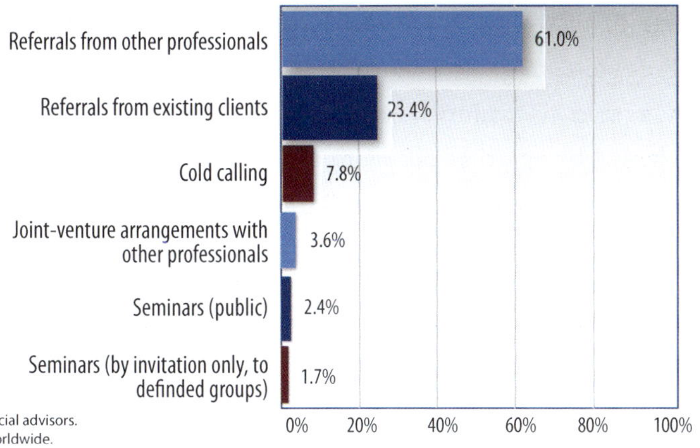

N = 2,094 financial advisors.
Source: CEG Worldwide.

It makes sense, then, that affluent clients want to find their financial advisors through referrals from professionals. In a study by Russ Alan Prince of more than 1,400 clients with a least $1 million in investable assets, 54.2 percent named referrals from professional advisors such as attorneys and accountants as an important way to find their primary financial advisors. Trailing behind in importance was referrals from existing clients of the financial advisor, cited by 30.1 percent of those surveyed. (See **Exhibit 2**.)

EXHIBIT 2
Importance in Finding a Primary Financial Advisor

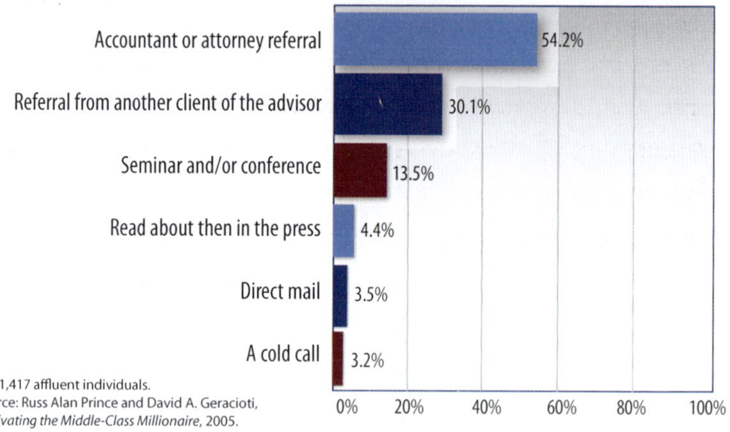

N = 1,417 affluent individuals.
Source: Russ Alan Prince and David A. Geracioti, *Cultivating the Middle-Class Millionaire*, 2005.

As important as referrals from other professional advisors are, we find that the great majority of financial advisors fail to maximize their relationships with these professionals. They may provide referrals to select professionals in the vague hope that they will receive reciprocal referrals. Or they may simply meet with other professionals and attempt to convince them that they are somehow different from all other financial advisors, and thus worthy of receiving their referrals.

Typically, these efforts bear very little fruit. Without a consistently compelling reason for the other professional to provide referrals to you, there is little that binds the relationship together over time. Even when referrals do trickle in, they can be of doubtful value. To build a highly successful practice, you do not need more *referrals* for just any prospects; however, you do need *introductions* to qualified future clients.

A well-crafted strategic alliance will give you exactly that. In contrast to informal referral arrangements, a strategic alliance creates a vested interest in each partner to help the other grow. An alliance creates "economic glue" that holds together a mutually beneficial partnership. It is a formalized ongoing relationship that has been clearly spelled out and committed to by both sides and sets the stage for a long-term profitable relationship for both parties.

Strategic alliances work, ultimately, because they enable you and your strategic partner to serve your clients better. Through the alliance, clients will benefit from both the expertise of the trusted professional with whom they already have a relationship and from your skills as a wealth manager who can address the full range of their financial concerns. And they can be assured that these professionals are working together as a team to maximize the probability that their clients achieve their financial goals.

And what is good for your clients, of course, is good for you. Our industry research has repeatedly shown that the top-earning financial advisors are much more likely than other financial advisors to have strategic alliances in place. Perhaps most important of all, strategic alliances will enable you to make a quantum leap in growing your business. We simply know of no better avenue for quickly moving upmarket and acquiring a whole new set of high-net-worth clients.

So strategic alliances hold the potential to greatly benefit both you and your future clients. But how would your potential strategic partners profit? In the next section, we will drill down on the most common type of alliance partner—CPAs—to see strategic alliances from their point of view. With this perspective, you will be well-equipped to approach professionals with assurance, knowing that you will be able to truly help them grow their businesses and serve their clients better.

The View from the Other Side

In 2009, CEG Worldwide carried out a comprehensive survey of CPA firms around the country that are offering financial services and products. One of our goals was to understand the mechanisms these CPA firms use to deliver financial services and products to their clients and the role of financial advisors in that delivery.

This has given us key insights into the importance of strategic alliances to CPAs. As you begin to approach potential strategic partners, this perspective will give you confidence that what you are proposing will be extremely valuable to those professionals.

To understand how the CPA firms are structuring their financial services practices, we segmented the survey respondents according to their service delivery model, or how they deliver financial services and products to their clients.

As **Exhibit 3** shows, we found that about one-third of surveyed firms (33.7 percent) use an internal model. That is, they provide all their financial services and products through one or more employees or partners at the firm. Just 1.0 percent of firms use an external model, whereby they provide all financial services and products through strategic arrangements with professionals outside the firm.

A sizable majority of the firms (65.4 percent) use a collaborative model, whereby they provide financial services and products through employees or partners and through strategic arrangements with financial services providers outside the firm.

EXHIBIT 3
Service Delivery Models of CPA Firms Offering Financial Services

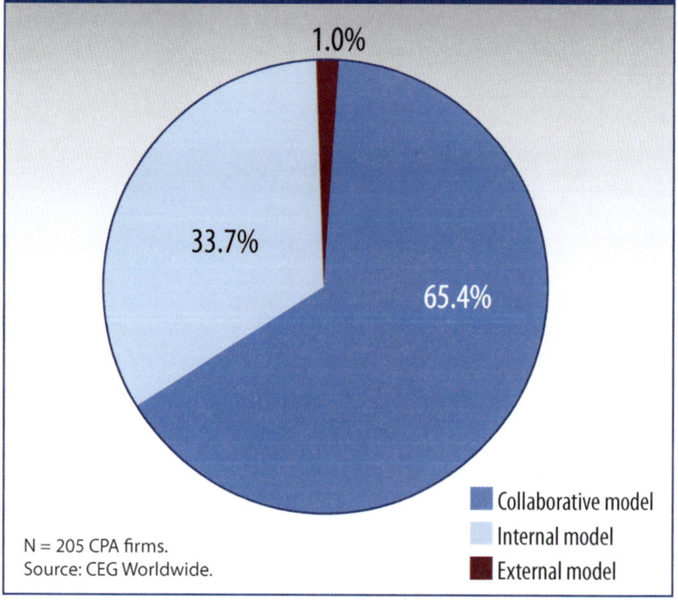

N = 205 CPA firms.
Source: CEG Worldwide.

We then dug deeper into the collaborative model to understand the types of outside service providers they use. As seen in **Exhibit 4**, the most common type of outside provider used by collaborative firms is the turnkey asset management program (TAMP). More than six in ten of surveyed collaborative firms, or 62.7 percent, rely on TAMPs for portfolio management and support. We believe that many of these CPA firms are attracted to TAMPs by their simple yet robust platforms that provide not just investment solutions but also assistance with practice management, operations and administration.

EXHIBIT 4

Use of Outside Providers by Collaborative Firms

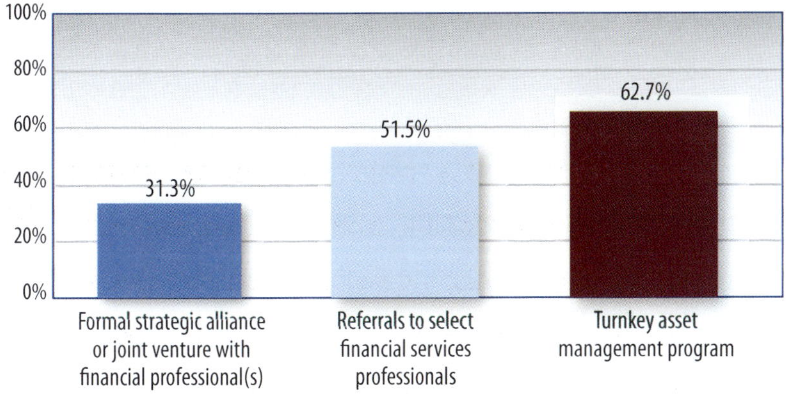

N = 134 CPA firms. Source: CEG Worldwide.

About half of collaborative firms (51.5 percent) provide clients with referrals to select financial services professionals to access financial services and products, while about one-third (31.3 percent) have created formal strategic alliances or joint ventures with one or more financial professionals. We believe that both of these provider types could be leveraged significantly more by collaborative firms, particularly as the value of strategic alliances with CPAs becomes more and more recognized by the major wirehouse firms.

To understand how each type of service model is succeeding, we looked at gross revenue from financial services and products for 2008. (Because so few firms use the external model—and a statistically insignificant sample from our study—we excluded them from this analysis.) We found that, regardless of the size of the firm, firms using the collaborative model earned significantly more on average from their financial services practices than firms using the internal model.

As **Exhibit 5** illustrates, the average revenue from financial services in 2008 for the firms using the internal model was $651,959 while financial services revenue for firms using the collaborative model topped $1 million.

EXHIBIT 5

2008 Gross Revenue from Financial Services and Products

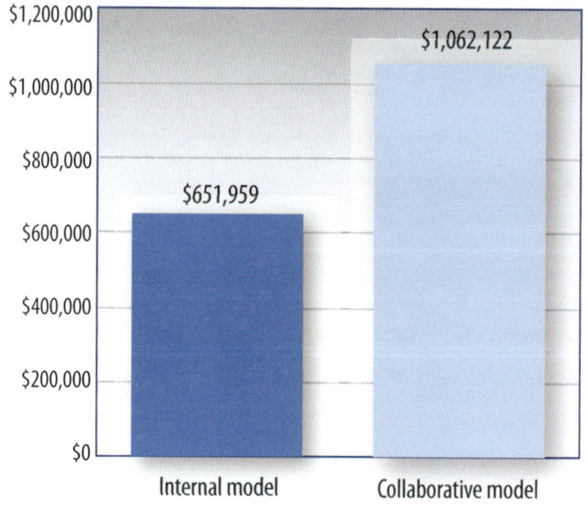

N = 203 CPA firms.
Source: CEG Worldwide.

We can assume that, because collaborative firms rely on outside professionals to deliver a portion of their financial services, their costs to provide these services is lower than for firms using the internal model. These lower costs would translate into higher profit margins on their gross revenues.

What accounts for the collaborative firms' higher earnings from financial services compared with firms that provide all financial services in-house? Above all, we believe it is their underlying embrace of strategic, collaborative relationships with outside professionals to deliver an optimal client experience.

We believe that these firms' willingness to turn to outside professionals comes primarily in response to market factors, including the greater complexity of financial products and increased client challenges due to market downturns and volatility. However, regardless of the reason, it provides financial advisors with significant opportunities to build profitable strategic alliances—and not just with CPAs. We will discuss the full range of your opportunities next.

Identifying Potential Partners

There are numerous types of professional advisors who can make excellent strategic partners. Among these, there are two types that stand out with their potential:

- **Accountants (CPAs)** whose clients include individuals and families in your target market can make excellent strategic alliance partners.
- **Attorneys** who work within your target market, particularly private client lawyers who specialize in trusts and estates and wealth protection, can also be extremely valuable strategic partners.

While strategic alliances with accountants and attorneys can be very powerful, your options do not end there. Consider these types of professionals:

- **Life insurance specialists** who work at the very high end of the market can have strong relationships with members of your target market. Importantly, they also have relationships with other professionals who serve the affluent, including private client lawyers, which can pave the way for additional opportunities for you.
- **Association executives** who lead organizations in your target market may be extremely open to exploring new ways to better serve their clients through a strategic alliance.
- **Business brokers** are open to strategic alliances with financial advisors because often the largest financial transaction that an affluent individual will make is the sale of his or her business. Business brokers know that many

transactions are not completed because the potential seller is unsure about how to invest the proceeds.

- **Investment bankers** who facilitate mergers and acquisitions are in a similar position as business brokers and may welcome a strategic alliance that helps clients to invest private equity that has been released.

- **Consultants** who work in your target market may have deep contacts that they can leverage to help you while further building their own businesses.

- **Casualty agents** who focus on the high end, specializing in multimillion-dollar homes or jets, for example, have the opportunity to build strong client relationships.

All these professionals share three important things in common:

- They work with affluent clients in your target market.

- They have the opportunity to build trusted, long-term relationships with their clients.

- They are interested in growing their businesses.

In this ebook, we focus special attention on accountants and attorneys. But keep in mind that the alliance-building process we describe can be used with virtually any type of professional advisor who has these characteristics.

With so many choices, how do you begin to narrow your options? As a first step, we recommend that you create a profile of what your ideal strategic partner would look like. Although you may not indentify an individual who perfectly matches this profile, it will help keep you on track toward the ideal through your discussions with candidates.

For example, your profile for the ideal CPA firm might look like this:

- Highly respected regional firm.
- Three to 20 CPAs in the firm.
- 150–300 clients per CPA.
- Principal specializes in your target niche.
- Principal is marketing-oriented and has a very entrepreneurial outlook.
- Firm is client-centric and focused on the best interest of its clients.
- Firm sincerely wants to help clients solve their problems and achieve their goals.
- Firm is open to working with other professional advisors.

And this may be the profile for the type of attorney you decide to work with:

- Works extensively with affluent clients.
- Works extensively with other professional advisors to the affluent.
- Specializes in trusts and estates, including wealth protection.
- Has a very entrepreneurial outlook and is marketing-oriented.
- Is interested in growing the firm's business in innovative ways.
- Has best interest of clients in mind.
- Sincerely wants to help clients solve their problems and achieve their goals.
- Shares your commitment to client service, integrity and professionalism.

Once you have created a profile of the ideal strategic partner, prepare a master list of candidates. To do so for accountants, turn to the *Business Journal* (www.bizjournals.com), which offers lists of leading firms in dozens of markets around the country. In addition, CPA Directory (ww.cpadirectory.com) has a searchable list of thousands of CPAs. You can also phone the heads of your local and state CPA societies to ask for assistance in identifying the leading firms in your market.

To create a list of attorney candidates, start with the attorneys of your wealthiest, most ideal clients. From these attorneys, identify those who serve the high end of the market with trusts and estates work. If none of your clients have relationships with this type of attorney, your second option is to contact the American College of Trust and Estate Counsel (www.actec.org) Likewise, any local organization that works in the estate planning area should be able to offer you leads.

Once your master list of candidates is complete, identify the top five possibilities. In the case of CPA firms, you need to assess the whole firm, although your primary contact will likely be the managing partner. For attorneys, you need look only at the individual attorney, not his or her entire firm.

Next, contact the potential partner directly. Tell him or her that you would like to discuss joint opportunities for working together and then schedule an exploratory meeting. These can be difficult calls for financial advisors to make, but in our experience, they nearly always receive a positive response from potential partners. There is a simple reason for this: These professionals need help with business development. They are facing real challenges in growing their practices.

Accountants in general have seen their consulting work fall considerably during the economic downturn. Their tax and audit work has remained the same or grown, albeit under tremendous price pressure—clients who never before negotiated fees are doing so now. So while firms may be bringing in the same revenue as before the downturn, they are netting less.

Private client lawyers face their own challenges. With the ongoing ambiguity and uncertainly around estate tax law, many affluent clients are reluctant to update their estate plans unless they absolutely have to. Without their more lucrative estate planning work, many private client lawyers are now just doing estate settlements.

Given such conditions, these professionals are pre-conditioned to work with financial advisors. Many, in fact, will be quite eager to meet with you. Remember this as you make your initial calls.

Once you have these initial meetings scheduled, you will be ready to begin the strategic alliance consultative process, which allow you to determine the right strategic partners and to launch your alliances effectively. We take an in-depth look at that process next.

The Strategic Alliance Consultative Process

WE BELIEVE THAT YOUR PROCESS FOR FORMING STRATEGIC alliances should be systematic and fine-tuned so that you can use it repeatedly to achieve consistently good results. It should be broken down into discrete steps with specific actions and desired outcomes for each.

The strategic alliance process we recommend is based around a series of meetings with strategic partners. (See **Exhibit 6**.) Each meeting is carefully designed to achieve specific goals and outcome, so do not be tempted to take shortcuts—we have found that they are the shortest route to failure in strategic alliances.

EXHIBIT 6
The Strategic Alliance Consultative Process

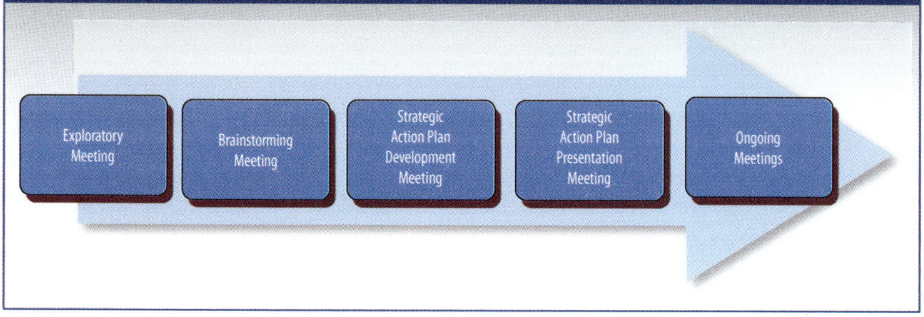

Exploratory Meeting

The purpose of this initial meeting with potential partners is to answer one fundamental question: Is this a good match? Your time is extremely valuable, so this meeting is designed to help you determine as quickly as possible whether the potential partner or firm is right for you and whether you should continue the consultative process.

We recommend that you take these three steps in each exploratory meeting:

1. Interview the candidate.
2. Explain the pyramid of relationships.
3. Make a decision and if appropriate, schedule the next meeting.

Interview the Candidate

Your first step is to capture all the information necessary to make a decision on whether to proceed further with the potential partner. The candidate will judge you by the quality of the questions you ask, so we suggest that you create an interview guide in advance of the meeting to ensure that you succinctly cover every major issue related to the strategic alliance.

We provide financial advisors who participate in CEG Worldwide's coaching programs with comprehensive interview guides for both CPAs and attorneys. These are some sample questions from those interview guides:

- What are the three key services that your clients are asking you for today?
- What are the characteristics of your ideal client?
- How do you differentiate yourself from your competition?
- What have been some of your biggest marketing successes?

As you move through your interview, drill down deeper where necessary to get the perspective you will need to make a decision about continuing to explore an alliance with the potential partner.

Explain the Pyramid of Relationships

Once the interview is complete and you have a good sense of how the other professional does business, move on to describe what your relationship would look like and exactly how it would benefit the potential partner.

To do so, we recommend that you frame the alliance with what we call the pyramid of relationships (see **Exhibit** 7). Besides presenting the alliance in a visual way—making it easier to quickly grasp—the pyramid of relationships unmistakably communicates your compelling value to the potential partner. By the time you have finished explaining the pyramid, the other professional will clearly see how you stand apart from other financial advisors and how you can benefit his or her business and clients.

EXHIBIT 7

The Pyramid of Relationships

Source: CEG Worldwide.

Show the other professional the diagram of the pyramid and begin your explanation with the bottom layer. The entire relationship rests on the foundation, which must have four key elements:

1. **Integrity:** Are both partners principled, trustworthy and reliable? Will you be able to fully trust one another?

2. **Chemistry:** Do you connect with each other on both a professional and personal level? Do you have genuine rapport?

3. **Empathy:** Do you understand one another's issues and challenges?

4. **Competence:** Do both partners have the professional experience and technical expertise required to capably address their clients' challenges?

These essential ingredients must be present for the alliance to be a success. If you feel that any are missing, you need not explore the relationship beyond this initial meeting.

Next move up the pyramid to the **collaboration** level. The other professional will absolutely need to know that clients that he or she introduces to you are being served very well. The best way to reassure him or her that that is the case is to spell out your wealth management consulting process, how the professional will introduce clients to the process and exactly how the clients will benefit from it.

In addition, describe how you and the other professional would work together collaboratively to address clients' advanced planning needs. In return for his or her work on your expert team, the professional would be paid a fair share for the value he or she delivers. (For detail on the wealth management consultative process and expert teams, please see **A Word About Wealth Management** on page 30.)

The third level of the relationship is **formalization**, or concurring on the fundamentals that will make the alliance work over time. By far the most important element is financial—the "economic glue" will hold the alliance together. In every case with a strategic partner, this glue will come at least in part from the growth of both businesses. In most cases, it will also involve a share of the revenue generated by the partner's clients.

Where there will be a revenue share, describe exactly what this could look like for the potential partner. For instance, for accounting firms, one rule of thumb says that there is $100 million of assets available per $1 million of accounting revenue. (In our experience, this rule generally works for accounting firms of up to $10 million in revenue.)

If the potential partner firm has $2 million in revenue, that would mean that its clients have about $200 million in assets. Assuming that you were able to capture those assets, it would generate $2 million per year in fees, assuming a 1 percent management fee. Of this, $500,000 would go to the accounting firm, assuming a very typical 25 percent revenue share. An additional $500,000 in revenue will no doubt be very attractive to the partner, especially since it would come at very little cost—simply the client introductions and the partner's work on your expert team.

In addition, the impact on the firm's valuation can be substantial. While accounting firms are currently valued at about 85 cents on the dollar of accounting revenue, the valuation for revenue streams from strategic partners are much higher—on the order of four to five times the revenue stream. Again, this will be highly attractive to potential partners, particularly those who are concerned about business succession issues and who are looking to bring younger partners into the firm.

Remember that this is just an exploratory meeting, so do not make any promises, especially about revenue, but do make the potential clear through reasonable hypothetical figures.

The top level of the pyramid is **best practices**. These are the specific actions you will take in collaboration with your strategic partner that will launch the alliance toward tremendous success. Your goals for these best practices are to effectively introduce the partner firm to your wealth management consultative process and create channels for the firm's clients to easily enter the process.

We recommend these three best practices to kick off strategic alliances:

1. Conduct a pilot program whereby the strategic partner and ten suitable clients go through your wealth management consultative process.

2. Conduct a second-opinion campaign to motivate additional clients of the partner firm to go through your consultative process.

3. Conduct a series of private events for clients of the partner firm.

Because these actions are crucial to the success of the alliance, we will cover each of them in some detail in the next section.

Make a Decision

Once you have finished discussing the pyramid of relationship, it is time to wrap up the meeting by deciding whether or not you should continue the strategic alliance consultative process with this potential partner. Evaluate what you have heard and trust your instincts. Remember that you are not committing to the alliance at this point, just to investing additional time with this potential partner.

If you decide to move ahead, schedule the next meeting in the process, the brainstorming meeting. Explain to your potential partner that you would like to meet with the other decision-makers in the firm in order to gain an understanding of what they will be open to and to collect more information for creating a strategic action plan.

Brainstorming Meeting

At this meeting, you will use the same interview guide you used at the exploratory meeting to gain insights from key partners at the firm. Listen closely and respond thoughtfully to the concerns that are raised. Make detailed notes of the conversation (or better yet, capture it with an audio recorder so that you can focus on the discussion). You will use these notes or the recording later when you create the strategic action plan.

In addition to giving you the chance to confirm whether you initial decision about this partner was correct, this meeting is your opportunity to communicate to the partners your consultative process and the value you offer to clients as a wealth manager.

Do not be surprised to encounter the "rule of thirds" at this meeting. We have found time and again a tendency for about one-third of partners at this meeting to be supportive of the proposed alliance, for one-third to oppose it and for the remaining one-third to be neutral about it. Do not be overly concerned about resistance at this point. We have found that a carefully crafted strategic action plan and, even more important, initial successes with client conversion go far toward winning over the opposition.

At the end of the brainstorming meeting, assuming that you still see substantial promise for a successful alliance, set up a follow-up meeting with your potential partner for the purpose of creating the strategic action plan.

Strategic Action Plan Development Meeting

The strategic action plan (SAP) will be the road map that moves your strategic alliance from concept to tangible success. It will be carefully scrutinized by your potential partners, so invest the effort necessary to make it powerful. It should clearly communicate these items:

- **An overview of your strategic alliance process.** Just as you communicate your wealth management consultative process to prospects and clients, you should communicate your strategic alliance consultative process to potential partners. Include an illustration such as that found in Exhibit 6 to graphically display the steps in the process.

- **Description of the challenges facing the potential partner.** Demonstrate your knowledge of the potential partner's business and industry by summarizing what you heard about the challenges during your exploratory and brainstorming meetings.

- **The benefits of the strategic alliance.** Spell out what a strategic alliance can mean for the partner, both in revenue and profit and in addressing the challenges you described. Importantly, it should also point out how the partner's clients will be better served through your wealth management consultative process.

- **Specific proposals for first steps.** Specify your recommendations for launching the strategic alliance. There should be no more than three, and each should be aimed directly at bringing qualified clients of the partner into your wealth management consultative process.

At your SAP development meeting, work with your potential partner to draft the document. Draw from notes you made during the exploratory and brainstorming meetings to make the plan as concrete and detailed as possible.

While your approach should be collaborative, you should lead the way in the creation of the SAP. We have found that the most efficient way to do this is to prepare a template of the plan in advance that contains the major sections you want to include with sample language. (CEG Worldwide provides such templates to participants in its coaching programs.) By the end of this meeting, you should have a plan that the potential partner fully supports.

Strategic Action Plan Presentation Meeting

At this meeting, you will present the strategic action plan to the decision-makers that you met with during the brainstorming meeting. Your goal is to show that you have a tremendous value to offer the firm and its clients, so prepare for the meeting thoroughly. Rehearse your presentation and polish both the written plan and accompanying PowerPoint presentation.

As you present the SAP, encourage discussion. Listen carefully for opportunities or objections that you may not have heard in your previous meetings. Be prepared to modify the plan accordingly. Endeavor to reach solid agreements about executing the recommendations you provide in the plan, with concurrence on timetables and on who will be responsible for each task.

Once you get agreement to move ahead, schedule the first of your ongoing meetings. Then begin immediately to execute the plan. It is extremely important to have some early successes in order for all stakeholders to remain committed, so work closely with your strategic partner to ensure that this happens.

Ongoing Meetings

At these meetings, you and your strategic partner will ensure that all the agreed-to items from the SAP are being executed. You will also assess your overall progress toward your goals and discuss opportunities for enlarging the alliance.

Constantly refer back to the plan and schedule ongoing meetings at an appropriate interval (such as twice a month or monthly) to make sure that you keep up with carrying out the actions outlined in the plan. Report successes often to all stakeholders to build and sustain momentum, and be ready to fine-tune the plan as you proceed.

After six months to a year, one of these ongoing meetings should include multiple partners from the firm to review overall progress (including revenue numbers) and to respond to any questions or issues that have arisen.

A Word About Wealth Management

During the exploratory meeting with potential strategic partners, be absolutely clear about your compelling value proposition, which is your ability to address the financial challenges of the other professional's clients through a comprehensive wealth management approach. This will clearly differentiate you from all the other financial advisors who approach the professional seeking simple referral agreements.

At CEG Worldwide, we define wealth management with this formula:

Wealth management = investment consulting + advanced planning + relationship management

Investment consulting is the core offering for many wealth managers and the foundation upon which they begin to build the client relationship.

Advanced planning addresses the four key areas of affluent clients' financial concerns beyond investments: wealth enhancement, wealth transfer, wealth protection and charitable gifting.

Relationship management focuses on client relationships, relationships with a network of financial professionals, and relationships with affluent clients' other professional advisors, such as attorneys and accountants.

In our coaching programs, we teach a wealth management consultative process that unfolds over a series of five meetings, not unlike the strategic alliance consultative process. Each meeting is designed to build deep client relationships while enabling the wealth manager to systematically serve clients extremely well.

An important tool for wealth managers is the expert team—a carefully chosen group of professional advisors who advise wealth managers on advanced planning issues. In addition to becoming your strategic partner, the other professional will also become a member of your expert team, lending his or her insight on important client cases.

Best Practices for the Strategic Alliance

WHETHER YOUR STRATEGIC ALLIANCES SUCCEEDS OR FAILS over the long term will largely be determined by how well you execute the three best practices you will recommend in your strategic action plan. Our experience working with financial advisors has shown that these three recommendations will effectively introduce the partner firm to your consultative process and create channels for the firm's clients to enter the process—if they are executed properly.

We focus next on each of these best practices and how to put them to work for your strategic alliance.

Conduct a Pilot Program

The first best practice that you should carry out is a pilot program that introduces your wealth management consultative process to two important groups.

First, your strategic partner and key partners at the firm should go through your consultative wealth management process. The only way for them to fully understand and appreciate the value of your process is to experience it first-hand. Position this exercise as an opportunity for the key partners to receive a second opinion on their financial situation while giving them direct experience of what they will be recommending to their clients—it is not about making the partners your clients.

Second, your partner should introduce you to ten of the top clients of the firm who are suitable for your services. He or she should frame it to the clients as an offer of a second opinion on their finances. Not only does this provide a genuine value to the clients, it gives your partner the opportunity to hear feedback from the clients on the quality of your service. Assuming that that quality is top-notch, this will motivate the partner to introduce additional clients to you.

Keep in mind that you are not agreeing to work with every one of the partner firm's clients. To be a top-tier wealth manager, you need clients with sufficient assets for whom you can provide substantial value. Sticking to your standards here also demonstrates to the partner firm that it, too, does not necessarily have to take every prospect who walks in the door.

Conduct a Second-Opinion Campaign

Together with your strategic partner, create a marketing campaign that motivates clients to go through your wealth management consultative process. The campaign should communicate three key messages:

1. The partner firm has joined forces with a leading wealth manager in order to offer clients an expanded range of services designed to address their full gamut of financial concerns.

2. As part of the strategic alliance, the wealth manager is offering clients a second opinion on their finances. There is no charge or commitment for this service.

3. Through the wealth manager's comprehensive consultative process, clients will receive a clear understanding of their current financial position and recommendations for what they should consider doing to achieve what is most important to them financially.

The best ways for the partner to reach out to clients will depend on the type of clientele and his or her relationship with them. They may include personal phone calls, letters and emails, brochures, a page on the firm's Web site, and a PowerPoint presentation for use during client meetings. Consider carefully the combination that will be most effective and, if appropriate, engage a marketing professional to ensure top quality. (CEG Worldwide offers these services and more for our coaching clients.)

Conduct Private Client Events

Presentations for the general public by financial advisors are not effective for drawing in qualified affluent clients. In contrast, thoughtfully designed private events for select invitees can be very positive for your business. When done in conjunction with a strategic partner, they can have an even greater impact.

Your goal with these events is twofold: The first is to draw qualified clients into your consultative process. The second is less obvious but still important: to have your strategic partner see you through the eyes of his or her clients. In this way, the partner sees the impression that your wealth management process and communication skills have on attendees.

These events should be by invitation-only for clients (and clients' friends and associates) of your strategic partner. Depending on your arrangement, invitations should be sent out directly from your partner or jointly by both of you.

As you plan your client events, remember that the content should be highly relevant to your audience. Wrap the concerns and issues of your partner's clients into your content in ways that capture the attention of the audience and shows them that you are highly qualified to manage their wealth. Just as important, your content should feel action-oriented and should motivate attendees to take you up on your invitation to enter your consultative process.

To make the positive impression you want, invest in high-quality presentation materials (such as the PowerPoint presentation and workbooks and other handouts) as well as marketing materials (including brochure, Web pages, emails and direct mail). This is another area where CEG Worldwide provides direct support to its coaching clients.

As you go about implementing these best practices, remember that strategic alliances will be successful only when your service is truly world-class. Your strategic partners have to hear that their clients are your raving fans. When they do, they will continue to introduce more clients. If they do not hear those endorsements, those introductions will dry up.

Tapping the Power

By now, we hope that you recognize the power of strategic alliances to significantly and rapidly expand the number of affluent clients you serve. To help you to realize this potential, we have provided you with some key tools:

- An understanding of the ability of strategic alliances to grow your business
- Insights into the importance of strategic alliances to the most successful CPA firms
- A process for determining the best potential partners for your strategic alliances
- The strategic alliance consultative process—a methodical, five-meeting process for building successful strategic partnerships
- The top three best practices for ensuring that your strategic alliances thrive from the beginning

To help you further, we have created a series of three videos that detail other critical aspects of strategic alliances and how to build them effectively:

- How to smoothly implement the strategic alliance consultative process and to maximize each of the five meetings with potential partners
- How to use the pyramid of relationship to win over reluctant potential partners and then to use it as a road map for a successful strategic alliance

- How **Breaking Through**—CEG Worldwide's intensive, yearlong coaching program for financial advisors—will assist you every step of the way as you form new strategic alliances

Do not leave your future up to chance. Be successful on purpose by forging strategic alliances in the right way with the right professional advisors. You, your strategic partners and your future clients will all be winners for it.

About CEG Worldwide

CEG Worldwide is the premier coaching, consulting and research organization for the financial services industry. We empower financial advisors to achieve breakthrough results in their careers by substantially increasing assets under management, affluent client acquisition and personal net income—all while serving their clients well.

We deliver insights into the best practices of elite advisors, garnered from empirical research, and coach advisors how best to implement these practices in their firms. The result is a focused, energized and enriched advisor who delivers client-centered services that build lifetime loyalty.

CEG Worldwide also works collaboratively with leaders of financial institutions to grow net new assets under management and the loyalty of their top financial advisors while attracting new top advisors. We provide insights, developed from empirical research, into what motivates top advisors, how to help them stay fully engaged and how to accelerate the achievement of their professional goals. Our services secure the long-term success and allegiance of top advisors who generate significant income for financial institutions.

About the Authors

John J. Bowen Jr.

CEO John Bowen founded CEG Worldwide in 2000, with the goal of bringing to bear the lessons he had learned during his career for the benefit of financial advisors and the institutions that work with advisors. His 26 years as a financial advisor and investment firm CEO had taught Bowen that many advisors lacked the high-quality empirical data and pragmatic business experience necessary to build hugely successful businesses. Bowen founded CEG Worldwide to fill that void, with the belief that providing advisors and institutions with research about the best practices of top elite advisors—and the coaching to use these practices effectively—would help them achieve new levels of success.

CEG Worldwide represents the culmination of Bowen's unique financial services industry experience. That experience encompasses a career as a financial advisor, including eight years as CEO of Reinhardt Werba Bowen Advisory Services, where he helped manage more than $1.6 billion in assets. Bowen sold that company and subsequently became CEO of Assante Capital Management, where he served as a member of the senior team as the firm more than tripled assets under management to more than $25 billion. Through these experiences, Bowen learned firsthand the best practices for substantial success. He also learned that the vast majority of advisors and institutions lacked a road map to build a simple and elegant practice—so he founded CEG Worldwide to provide other advisors and institutions the lessons his experience had taught him.

Bowen is widely recognized as a leader in the financial services industry. He writes a highly acclaimed monthly column for the leading U.S. financial services trade journal, *Financial Planning*. He is the author or co-author of several books, including *Breaking Through: Building a World-Class Wealth Management Business*, *The Prudent Investor's Guide to Beating Wall Street at Its Own Game* and *Creating Equity: How to Build a Hugely Successful Asset Management Business.*

Bowen received his BS degree in economics from the State University of New York Fredonia, an MBA in taxation from Golden Gate University and a master's degree in financial services from The American College.

Paul Brunswick

Paul Brunswick brings proven sales, coaching and leadership skills to the CEG Worldwide team. He has extensive financial services experience and a proven track record working with both institutional and ultra-high-net-worth clients, as well as with financial advisors and branch managers. Brunswick has both field and corporate expertise in developing talent at all levels within a financial services organization.

Brunswick has had more than 20 years of success in the financial services industry. Most recently, he was the director of national business development for Smith Barney, where he provided strategic and tactical direction to the firm's entire private client distribution channel. He led campaigns designed to increase advisor net asset flow, grow fee-based revenue and improve advisor competency in such key areas as investment and wealth management. He also had responsibility for internal communications, new product approval and the research strategy group.

Earlier, he worked at Smith Barney in a variety of management positions across the country. He started his financial career as a financial consultant for Merrill Lynch in St. Louis, Missouri.

Jonathan J. Powell

Jonathan Powell's considerable expertise in developing top-performing financial advisors is a great asset to the clients he serves through CEG Worldwide. Working with many of the nation's top financial firms, he enjoys helping advisors transform their professional and personal lives by using CEG Worldwide's research-backed principles.

Powell has hired and coached hundreds of the industry's top financial advisors—in multiple distribution channels—for more than 25 years. After starting his career as an independent financial planner in the San Francisco Bay area, he went on to spend more than two decades with Citigroup before retiring to pursue his passion for training and coaching.

In his lengthy career, Powell has managed branches for Smith Barney and led Citibank's West Coast brokerage business, overseeing 290 financial advisors and 20 managers. While at Citigroup, Powell was a sought-after speaker for national and regional conferences on topics including time management, financial advisor strategies for success and effective recruiting.

Powell earned a BA in economics from Stanford University and holds the CFP designation. He is a co-author of *Breaking Through: Building a World-Class Wealth Management Business.*

Printed in Dunstable, United Kingdom

91342916R00027